Journey

For Dona,
long time friend
(and long-ago colleague)
with best wishes
and love,

Lilly

ALSO BY LILLY BARNES

FICTION
A Hero Travels Light
Mara

CHILDREN'S FICTION
Lace Them Up
Make it Better

CHILDREN'S NON FICTION
Toe Tapper

Journey

POEMS BY

Lilly Barnes

Inanna Poetry & Fiction Series

Inanna Publications and Education Inc.
Toronto, Canada

Copyright © 2014 Lilly Barnes

Except for the use of short passages for review purposes, no part of this book may be reproduced, in part or in whole, or transmitted in any form or by any means, electronically or mechanically, including photocopying, recording, or any information or storage retrieval system, without prior permission in writing from the publisher.

Canada Council for the Arts   Conseil des Arts du Canada

ONTARIO ARTS COUNCIL
CONSEIL DES ARTS DE L'ONTARIO
50 YEARS OF ONTARIO GOVERNMENT SUPPORT OF THE ARTS
50 ANS DE SOUTIEN DU GOUVERNEMENT DE L'ONTARIO AUX ARTS

The publisher gratefully acknowledges the support of the Canada Council for the Arts and the Ontario Arts Council for its publishing program, and the financial assistance of the Government of Canada through the Canada Book Fund.

The publisher is also grateful for the kind support received from an Anonymous Fund at The Calgary Foundation.

THE CALGARY FOUNDATION

Barnes, Lilly, author
    Journey : poems / by Lilly Barnes.

(Inanna poetry & fiction series)
ISBN 978-1-77133-146-3 (pbk.)

    I. Title. II. Series: Inanna poetry and fiction series

PS8553.A7628J68 2014   C811'.54   C2014-902099-6

Printed and bound in Canada

Inanna Publications and Education Inc.
210 Founders College, York University
4700 Keele Street
Toronto, Ontario, Canada M3J 1P3
Telephone: (416) 736-5356 Fax (416) 736-5765
Website: www.inanna.ca
Email: inanna.publications@inanna.ca

*for
Martin Roher
with Love, always*

Contents

1. Pains of Childhood

I do know what they mean	3
Don't Tell	4
Bunnies	10
Whose Enemy? Whose Liberator?	12
Making Angels	13
It Doesn't Show	15
Thanks, Tom	16
Just because I'm bigger	17
The Day My Mother Died	18
Unshed Tears	20
The Mystery	22
Ditty: After the Dark: Opus #1	24

2. The Journey

Ready or not	27
Leaving Behind	29

A Ripple	31
"Knock Knock"	32
The little demon that could	36
The Fear of Heights	40
Marvellous Despair	44
Rainbow Girl	46
I am a Sponge (the gnarled-looking one plucked from the bed of oceans)	49
Singing	50
The Dancing Tree	51
Joy	53
A Birthday Poem	54
Will to Completion	55
Ditty: I'm Flying: Opus #2	57

3. The Joys of Age

There was a time	61
Footprints in the Clouds	62
There's a poem coming	64
Your Task, Your Joy	66
I'm Croning	69
Gentle Hands	71

This Moment	72
Perched	73
Something is coming	74
Behold	75
Loon Song	77
Dreaming	78
Stillness	80
Solitude	81
Ditty: There's a bug in my Soup, Opus #3	82
Acknowledgements	85

1

Pains of Childhood

I do know what they mean

Peel off white knee socks,
white shoes and the ribbons in my hair,
peel off the pinafore dress and matching lace panties,
slip on the bathing suit,
all naked arms and legs,
and out into the summer rain.

Run like a deer,
down the hillside to the bottom
where the mud is slick and silky warm.
Sit in it,
right in the middle,
with trickles of running rain water
and glistening pebbles,
and shape and pat and squish and wiggle,
and the slurpy tongues of mud between your toes

and nobody saying: Dirty!
Look what you've done to your clothes!

It happened only once.
Once in a life time, but it happened.
When people talk about their happy childhood,
I do know what they mean.

Don't Tell

Don't tell your mother has a secret.
Don't tell you don't know what it is.

Don't tell your ration cards were confiscated,
that your mother trades piano lessons
for butter and sausages,
that the parcels from your father
are full of canned sardines.

Don't tell you like Oskar,
he has dark hair and eyes
and his skin never burns in the sun.

Don't tell Herrman we hid his soccer ball or he'll kill you.
And don't tell anybody Ruth saw a picture of your grandfather
and said he looks Jewish.
Don't tell the next day your mother
burned all the photographs of her family.

Don't tell that your mother's friend
checked if you have breasts.
Maybe doctors always do that
but don't tell.

Don't tell anybody you saw the teacher

giving pears
to the man without ration cards.
Don't tell you can't remember why you're not allowed
to go swimming with Ruth.

Don't tell you're afraid of the war prisoner because
he might come and stab you in the night
for sticking out your tongue at him because
he was watching you skip,
trying to see your underpants.

Don't tell anybody you and the other children
ski down the bomb crater
that's much too steep
you might break your skis.

Don't tell about your dreams,
blood spurting out of the hole
in the farmer's face,
shot right off his wagon seat.
Don't tell, because it wasn't a dream.
And don't tell who rushed to the wagon
to grab the carrots the farmer was bringing into town.

Don't tell Monika rubs stuff on her lips and cheeks

so the boys will pull her braids.
Don't tell you stole three candy
and arranged the rest so nobody would find out.
Don't tell it was you because it's not the candy,
it's that you disobeyed.

Don't tell Mr. Schmidt fell down the basement stairs
because he was drunk.
He was supposed to be on air raid duty.
Don't tell anybody Lieselotte goes in his place,
dragging her clubfoot and crying.
It's true everybody knows, but don't tell.

Don't tell you can't figure out what's down there
even with a mirror
because it doesn't look anything
like the way it feels
when you're rocking in the bath tub.

Don't tell you saw Mr. Mueller take off his leg
and lean it against the tree
and rub his stump and cry.

Don't tell your mother recites Pushkin by the page
and drinks her tea through a cube of sugar.
Don't tell your mother listens to the radio speak Russian and English,
late at night.

Don't tell you're not afraid of the bombs
that you like the nights spent in the basement shelter

everybody snug together, with candles, like a family.

Don't tell you saw Ingrid under the lilac tree
accepting cigarettes from the American soldier.
She might get all her hair shaved off.

***

Don't tell you don't know why
your mother put you on this ship
to Israel.
Don't tell you don't know why
everybody has numbers tattooed
on their arms.

Don't ask questions.

Don't tell you don't know why
pulling the boy's cap off his head
is a crime.

Don't tell you can only speak German.
Don't tell anybody you can speak.

Don't tell you can see them
staring at you.
Don't tell you can see
the hate in their eyes.

Don't tell your suitcase is full of vomit.

Don't tell you stay on deck
because they might kill you in the cabin
while you're sleeping.
Don't tell you're thirsty
they might poison the water.

***

Don't you dare tell you're homesick
for your mountains,
they're in Germany.
You're in Israel now.
What are you, the devil's child?

Don't tell anybody your father is German.
Don't tell anybody he is Catholic.
Pretend he is dead.

Don't tell anybody you used to have a scooter
and skis, and roller skates
presents from your father.

Don't tell it was Lieselotte
who brought baskets of apples and bread
to eat with your sardines.

Don't tell you love Beethoven
and Marzipan ladybugs hanging from the Christmas tree.
Don't tell you love horses racing and soccer games,

and women shelling peas in the courtyard,
gossiping.

Don't tell that you can't sleep because
you might talk in your dreams
in German.

Don't tell anybody that sometimes
you forget who you're supposed to hate.

Don't tell Sarah it's not that she's black
and homesick for Morocco.
Don't tell her you can't be friends because
you might get careless
and tell her secrets.

There is no Truth and Reconciliation Committee here.
There's only death by gag
stuffed down the gullet and deep into the belly
festering.

Bunnies

When the war is over, they said
We will have chocolate Easter bunnies

But the only bunnies left are Lieselotte's
The white angora rabbits, pinky-eyed
The ones she cradles
When she's crying.
Or scolds, when they try to leave
Her mother lap.

She always talks to the littlest one
In whispers
She calls it by her dead son's name.

I had a bunny once
A birthday present from my father far away
I called it Honey Lamb
And cuddled it too hard
And took it everywhere.

And then it disappeared
My Honey Lamb
And mother said to stop the fussing
Because it was the first in many months
That stew with real meat, last Sunday.

So only Lieselotte's bunnies are still here
For covering up with Easter chocolate
But maybe they are lucky bunnies
Maybe the war will never end.

Enemy? Liberator?

Our Liberators, said my mother and dissolved in tears.
Now we'll be free to leave.

Leave? Leave home?

They're here. They're here.
All the kids in my neighborhood
running down to the crossroads.
Jeeps, tanks, trucks rolling by
full of smiling soldiers.

They're pointing guns
there's still fighting in the mountains
between the children's fathers and the soldiers

With the other hand, they smile and throw candies.
All the children scrabble on the ground,
pushing and grabbing.

Everbody except me.
I stand up straight and stiff,
unbending.
Somebody has to show some pride and dignity in defeat
even if it's me, the black-haired girl with a Russian mother.
The one, they say, who never once gave the Hitler salute.

Making Angels

A bag of chestnuts
hoarded
tied on our back
and we're off

Powder snow
silence
no foot prints anywhere
the trees majestic
tall straight trunks of pines
Honourable

We climb for hours to reach the mountain's top
and here we rest
waiting
ready

The first to show are eyes
eyes of doe
and snout
wet and warm, when it reaches your palm
gently pulling the chestnut from your hand

The others follow, one by one.
The grand old buck stands motionless at the forest edge

antlers high and watchful

And then they're gone,
melting into the forest
and we're happy
slapping ourselves warm
bracing for the descent

Like the wind, we ski
swirling round and around the mountain
like wild devils we whoop
released from school, from being good little children
like wood sprites we emerge from the forest
at the bottom of the mountain
and fall into a heap on the snow
skis sticking up every which way
and arms beating like wings
making angels

It doesn't show

Your birth certificate, please.
It's in Russian, I say.
I can't even read it, I never could.

But the woman has no mercy:
I can, she says. *I will.*

I hand over the tattered yellow document,
and watch her eyes fly down the page.
No sudden pause
not a muscle moves in her face
it's clear, the truth about me is not written here:

Born: unwanted
Ruined her mother's life.

Thanks, Tom

My mom read me a bedtime story
Her voice was soft and gentle low
She had one arm around my shoulder
hugging me close all the way to
The End.

Then she gave me a kiss and said
Good night, my beloved little girl,
and left my bedroom door open
all night long.

So okay. That never happened.
So okay, I'm making it up.
But it's like Tom Robbins told us:
Never too late, he said.
It's never too late to have a happy childhood.

Just because I'm bigger

There's a bat in my bedroom
Oh, shriek
Oh, shiver

From under the sheets I watch its shadow flutter
disoriented
afraid

Both of us quivering
both of us panicked
but the way out is up to me.
Why me?

The Day My Mother Died

Scared of cats in my bed climbing on my chest,
suffocating me while I sleep,
of bats in the basement or under the roof
spreading enormous wings to blot out the light,

Scared of getting my white clothes dirty and my mother
saying I was giving her another migraine,
of playing the wrong note on the piano and getting
the lid slammed on my hands
like the little girl fetching an apple out of the bin and her stepmother
slamming the lid shut on her neck and the little girl's head
rolling among the apples.
I'm scared my mother will leave me alone again
this time forever.

I'm scared to make a sound when the dressmaker sticks pins in me,
I'm scared to cry when I miss my dad,
scared to laugh, sounding just like my father,
scared he'll find out I ruined my mother's life.

Scared of the blind piano tuner's stick
he doesn't understand "out of sight, out of mind."
He pokes me out of my hiding place under the dining room table.

I'm scared to be friends with Helga because she asks a lot of questions.
I'm scared of finding my suitcase, packed, standing beside my bed
in the morning.

Fears riding me
through all the days and nights and years
until
my mother died.

Unshed Tears

I never cried when the forget-me-nots disappeared
nor when my father stopped visiting at Christmas
and I wasn't allowed to open his parcel.

I never cried for Hans, my first love,
who carried me home piggy-back when he was 17
and I was 5
and fully intended to marry him one day.
I never cried when they said "killed in action"
and his mother went mad with grief.

I never cried when I was sent away,
to live at the children's home,
to wait
or when the kittens were taken from us because
they didn't belong in a home.

I didn't cry, torn from one country after another,
leaving best friends behind forever,
pulled and pushed across continents,
languages,
landing willy nilly
and perched for years in expectation of another move.
I never cried to have no place called home.

Mementos of my life,
fill every nook of my house.
Hoarded, useless, clutter.
Every memento an unshed tear.

Lately, I sit and weave,
pulling together the strands of my life
across the whoof and warp of time,
calling up names and following their threads
picking at the lint of memory.

This year, forget-me-nots came into my garden
and I cried and cried,
for happiness,
and all the unshed tears.

The Mystery

The fragrance is a mystery.
Surely not the half dead gardenia?

From beneath gas fumes
and odours of the city
it sneaks into my being
like a still living memory
and lingers
recalling all the times of flowers
which weave in and out of life
and bring forever more
the Mystery.

Speak not of seasons
or of all the many days now past
They take too long in the enumerating
when all my attention
wants to stay here
with the fragrance of mystery.

When did you last encounter
that subtle silent joy
found when not searching
but only opening your heart
to the abundance of the universe

and all its gifts.

Breathe deeply, while it lasts
and bathe yourself in all there is…

There, now you've got it
never to be lost
and when you next encounter
the void, the darkness of the night
you'll still be bathed
and clamoring
and floating out and up
on wings
elusive and undeniable
as the fragrance of gardenias.

That's what is meant by being open
to the joys at hand
and winging it.
That's what it is,
when you're alive to every moment's gift
That's what we call
the Mystery.

Ditty: After the Dark: Opus # 1

There's a bee in my bonnet
There's a monkey on my back
There's a grin on my face, I've
gone to hell and I've come back

Not for me the sad long faces
of the burial cemet'ry
I'm alive and I'll go dancing
Long as you will play with me.

I've achieved a peaceful dying
By my living to the hilt
And I don't intend to shiver
When the scythe descends on me
It's a ditty I am singing
It's a march for happy feet
Be it given by my own voice
Or the buzzing of a bee.

There's a bee in my bonnet
There's a spring in my step
I've no tears to shed this morning
Been to hell and now I'm back.

2.
The Journey

Ready or not

So, sweety. Ready yet to sail?
Your suitcase is packed.
You're off.

But I can't lift it.

I sink under the weight.
Nobody taught me to swim.
At the bottom
sharp rocks
but it's ground, at last, under my feet.

Breathing is shallow, here
You have to grow a shell
You learn to navigate.

Survival of the unfit.
Fitting is not possible.
A thicker shell. But breathing…

In the end you die.
Or, choosing life,
break open.
Unprotected.
Tears spring forth and carry you

up and up
you're buffeted and drifting
towards the shallows.

But Love.

Love beckons from beyond the deep,
with sun bedappled.
And now, with all your strength
you do set sail.
You're ready!

Leaving Behind

Leaving behind
like abandoned outworn skin
all the loathsome fears
all the wiles of the intrepid
wanderer in search of courage.
Leaving behind
in the grey dust and ashes
the awe-some, the awful,
the awe of the ape –
we're moving on, they cry
we're human, after all,
there's nothing truly awesome
any more.

Leaving behind
the gates to the city and lights
culling the countryside for stars
still remaining
the sky-filled air and dreams
of long lost ways.
Leaving behind also
the babes of the woods
who fear only the rushing and yowling
of coyotes and humans
on the hunt.

Finding, finally
the peace of surfeit
in the brook, the stream,
the dew of the morning
the joy of the shining stars
and the song of the wind.

Finding, above all,
the song of the heart
as it recovers its awe-struck
delight
in the gurgle of brooks and babies
the arms enfolding,
and love embracing the whole of it
the universe
which can be shaped for joy
or fear
and which, leaving behind
the outworn dry old skins
of never-in-awe
you can encounter all a-new
as you lift and soar
on wings of wonder.

A Ripple

Where the shadows of clouds hide in the lake
There breezes gather in a circle dance
Then, fanning out, a rippled smile
Across the water
They come to tease
And to invite you to the dance

A secret rippling in the blood
Is quick to answer
But all the rest is heavy
Disinclined to move
From the perch of comfort

The smile has disappeared
The breeze died out
The clouds form a blanket
Hiding all shapes

And the ripple in the blood
Just gas, I guess, excuse me, dear.
Did I really fall asleep again
I think I dreamt…

"Knock Knock"

Not a chance, she said
looking at my gnarled tree root fingers.
Not a chance they'll let you come in here.
You're much too tall,
too strong,
too full of sap for anyone
to see and to believe.
Not a chance, she said and snickered.

As if I'd asked to come inside.
I'm outdoor born and outdoor bred
and to uproot me from my land
is to deliver me to death
in all my cells.
I'm of the sky and air and soil
not indoor life,
I'm free.

Then why the knocking at my window?
Why knock with every breeze that comes
to whisper in the night?

I'm curious, that's all.
I want to hear and see
more of your goings on, in there.

There's so much yet to learn
about you two-foot creatures,
always running here and there,
then flopping down, with eyes a-glaze
to stare and watch as others run
on tiny screens
while all the time,
the bird that sings to me
the breeze and I
just stay out here and marvel.

We can't imagine how you live:
no roots, no leaves,
a skin that comes and goes,
and yet, there's life in there,
I hear it in your voices,
calling: Oh, god, where are
my gloves today? The keys?
The lunchbox, Freddy, here,
give us a kiss,
now run run run…

The sky is fathomless and deep
The stars are high and everywhere
The voices of our ancestors

are singing in the air.
But two foot creatures hear them not,
they're running to and fro
yet when they flop, or eat or sleep,
they're murmuring to us:
we're lost,
knock on the window, please,
do knock
and bring us news of roots and leaves
and sky and stars we cannot see.
Please sing to us
so we can dream of them,
so we can wake refreshed again
to start another day.

And so we do,
we knock and sing
and in your dreams
we dance, as well
high in the clouds and
deep beneath the ground
We keep the faith
that life is going on
just underneath the surface
of your days of running.

You see now why I knock and knock
it's up to me to keep awake, in dreams
what you forget on waking

and yet remember in some hidden singing breath
deep in your soul.

You're fascinating, you
You're unbelievable
You make us smile
and shiver, you:
another aspect of the mystery of life.

Knock knock
Who's there?
It's me, your dear beloved
with fingers gnarled as roots
and crown of leaves,
wispering songs to dream on
songs of love.

Now up you get,
knock knock, it's time
to start your running.

The little demon that could

What ancient stuff is this
rearing its head out of the distant past
so long buried, so deep and far away
I can hardly glimpse it:
a horrid head, a tail a-swishing
the color red – as anger –
it's a demon I've not been introduced to yet.

His name?

Has he no home except in me
my bones and marrow getting clogged
with his foul breath.
He sits and smirks in peace
a sentry at his door
keeps watch and says: no entry here
to anyone who knocks.

I know him now,
his name is legion but in me,
inside of me,
he's anger balled into a fist and,
smirking less,
he's recognized at last
and now he'll be uncovered more and more.

He'll yelp and whine and threaten, too
but he'll be shrivelling in every breath I take
with knowledge of his presence.
He'll not escape me now
I've got his name and number.

He'll squirm and flail
he'll scream, when all else fails
but he'll be dragged and pulled
and brought into the light
and then he'll squirm for sure
because there's nowhere left to hide.
He'll shrink and fade and soon
be wafted by a breeze
away and out and gone.

If you could see him now,
a-dancing in the breeze –
it's wonderful out here, he'll call
I didn't know!
There's light and air and colors and
there's movement, flow,
and joy, to be released.
I have no need for hiding ever more
and you, well, bon voyage, my dear

You've been my savior, all unknown
as we once were, to one another.

We're now apart
and free to come or go,
to be a-dancing on a breeze
or on a cloud…
Give us a kiss good bye, I say
we've done with one another.
We're parting friends because,
you see, we were so close
for such a time
we're kin, though parted,
you and I. We're free to choose
our future.

So as for me, I'm off to other realms
And you can shape your days just as you like
without that demon fist with horns and tail
without the red hot anger in your bones
And what will you, I wonder
put into its place?
Oh, that's quite clear –
where air and light have entered,
it's joy comes streaming in.

That's all quite clear and certain now,
I see it in your dancing step
and smile and eyes that shine.

So long again,
sweet parting, bon voyage
and may we be reminded now and then
of days and nights when all our trav'lling was together
in pain and tears
and may we be reminded now and then
of our sweet parting
and the sweetest sound of all:
of joyful laughter in the light.

The Fear of Heights

The fear of heights is in my bones
It keeps me huddled in this cave
Where ground is crawley things
And air is stench

It's not the fear of falling, see
It's not the fear of flying
It's merely fear of being high
Above the level ground
Where people dwell in safety
And rarely lift their eyes
To wonder at the mountain tops
And eagles in their flight

It's fear of being high above
The scurrying people who
Must surely know just how to live
To keep so serious a mien
And be so sure of every step
To have the answer to all
Questions on their tongue

If I were high as clouds or eagles
Think what I might see from there
But, no. Don't even dream of it

You'd be a freak, a silly goose
A female gone berserk
You'd be the one they whisper of
And you'd be so alone
With no one who would listen to
The tale of heights and vistas wide
As all the sea.

So huddle in your cave and
Call it fear of heights
And you'll be deemed acceptable
By all the civilized
Good people who are huddled, too
And crunching over bones
And breathing stale and fetid air
And never looking up
To see the stars.

Or wait, here is another thought
Get out of there and look
What other ways there are to live
What else there is to see
Explore, both in and out of caves
Examine every clue
To other paths

And don't forget to ask for help
From all the ancient ones:

Who knew to climb out of the cave
Who knew to fly and soar
Who knew the song which brings us
Rain and flowers
Who knew that fear is death in life
Who stepped along, quite gingerly
But moving forward all the time

And don't forget to ask your limbs
Your heart and eyes and ears
To guide you on this journey and
To keep you safe as you encounter
The ogres and the gods and goddesses
The obstacles and mine fields of the mind

And as, at length, you reach the place
Of vistas wide and rushing winds
To be at ease, at peace, alone, and
Joyful yet, and soon behold
That others have been climbing, too
And are entranced like you
At all the vastness of the view
And all the beauty of the world

And so you take a deeper breath
And swell your breast with love
For all the children who will see

And climb, because it's possible
Look, she's already there, so we can, too, let's go
Let's out of here and fast
Who needs this stench and crawley ground
And off they run and climb and call
And shriek with joy when they behold the world

So there you are
Your fear long gone
The cave a distant past
You're high among the mountain peaks
You're growing wings to fly
And all about you are the ones
Who also left behind
The fear and all its fetters and
The downcast eyes and minds

Hail Thee, our joyous guides, our heroines
Our gods and goddesses galore, *salud*
We're coming, too, to be with you
As soon as we are done
With sweeping, brushing, rushing to and fro
And filling up the tank
And – well – you know.

Marvellous Despair

Despair is silent, inward turned
it raises nothing, is barely breathing
stifled by unshed tears.
Deep in the darkest corner, it slumps
without hope.

And there you sit and wonder as the world goes on
paralysis o'ertaking every move
you watch the roil and toil of life as from afar
though your corner be right in the midst of it
you watch and ask youself, how can it be,
the world goes on,
have they not eyes to see?

You raise an eyebrow, squint
at the ray of light, try to catch
a glimpse of how it can all go on,
willy nilly, pell mell, no screams,
barely a frown,
busy as ants, rushing about.

Curious, you emerge
a tentative step forth from your darkest corner,
looking for signs, for reasons,
for the source of the strength

to keep on going.
You step out further,
curioser and curioser, and nothing tells you
what you want to know,
but willy nilly, pell mell,
next thing you know,
you're doing it, too:
moving around,
washing something, crying
over a paper cut,
blowing your nose
and then, you catch a glimpse
of despair
still hovering in the darkest corner,
paralyzed by the weight of no-hope,
and you pity it, and sigh,
and then you move
move on
and moving, you feel moved to seek
and quest
and then to marvel,
at all the multitudes of goings on, in life,
and marvelling,
you think it marvellous.

Rainbow Girl

Lost long ago
amidst bombs and threatening debris -
lost but not dead.

She sits at the end of a rainbow
filled with wonder and delight
she calls you, listen:
I'm here – I'm lost
please find me.

Look for her in the first blossom of spring
look for her in the spring of your step
when birds call from tree tops
and leaves unfurl to the sun.

Look for her in quiet moments
when only your breath is heard
and your heart beats
with love of the universe.

Look for her then and hear her voice
and call to her – she'll come
to hold your hand in wonder
at the long lost home you are,

at the love in your heart
still beating.

Look for her in dreams
when meadow flowers beckon
and wish on the first one you see
for the Rainbow girl,
still waiting.

You can't entice her with words,
with presents or pretty things
You can listen to her with your heart
and send out your loving breath
and she'll glide on it
as on a rainbow
back to her home
to you.

She's your own Rainbow girl
hold her hand
and lead her into your life
full of wonder and delight
in the living universe.

The stars shining brightly
and winking
their song on the evening breeze
are the gifts she'll accept
and delight in,
are the wonder you'll share
like a lullaby soft
and murmuring
as you drift into dreams
together
at home in your heart.

I am a Sponge (the gnarled-looking one, plucked from the bed of oceans)

I am a Sponge
Soaking up each moment
Until I'm full to over flowing.
A trickle, in the first beginning
And then a pouring
Into every river bed
Long dried by fear
And by withholding,
Now filling with elixir,
The overflowing moments,
Of my life.

A sponge?, you say
Oh, how mundane
How not up-lifting, lofty or poetic
How very ordinary.

Pish-tosh, my friend, I say
You go ahead: be lofty,
Labor to up-lift and to attain.
I am a sponge.

Singing

A motor boat can sing
its ebb and flow blending

with the sound of waves, ongoing
under and over it all.

A mosquito sings -
sometimes just up to the sound of slap
but it sings.

The basil plant on my railing
sings quietly all through the night
humming its growing song.

And then there's the rain on the roof
and the last chirping grasshopper in the tree…

You're never alone, if you're listening.
Never without song.

The Dancing Tree

The song of the lake
The silence of ducks
Swimming by in pairs
Panorama of sky and
Ever-shifting shapes of clouds
And me, a part of it, and breathing.

Beside me, Dancing Tree
Her branches whispering 'resilience',
Her leaves shimmering,
Her trunk encrusted
Gnarled with age
And me, a part of it, and breathing.

On the far shore
A boat is droning
In the treetops, a bird
Too small to see but talkative,
A rock, submerged by waves
Plays peek-a-boo
And me, a part of it, and breathing.

A drop of rain goes plop
A smudge decides to spread
It's time to flee, to cover up

To sigh and re-assemble
The parts which fit into my skin
And those which memory contains
In me, a part of me, and breathing.

Joy

Sometimes I remember
   in the abundance of wildflowers after the rain
   in the sound of trees
   as a white-capped wave riding the lake

   dust-bathing my feathers as a sparrow
   climbing the rusting gate as a vine
   drifting across the sky in ever-changing shapes of clouds

   cradling a baby
   a newborn song
   a dying lover

Sometimes I forget.

A Birthday Poem

Whitecaps
whipping across the lake
wild in refusal of formation
flying to the rocky shore
spraying silver into the blue
of sunlit sky.

Hillsides of Trees in motion
waves of gold and red
and all the hues of green
my heart is moaning to expand

And now the clatter of geese overhead
reminds of change
in the seasons of life.

The Will to Completion

Sitting in my drawer there's a manuscript
It whispers to me nightly:

I grew in your hands
I changed at your commmand
I moved and roiled and jumped through hoops
until you pronounced me done and
stuck me in a drawer.

And here I lie, incarcerated
never born
no light, no air, no voices murmuring
in praise or approbation.
Flat lying pages where my life should be
Flat printed marks where words should fly from eye to heart
Abandoned. Left to rot and molder
the juices of my life dried up.

Who will unearth me?

There must have been an urge
once loud and clear
to have me loosed upon the world
to bring delight, inform, be loved, and hated, too

to join the dance and swing from hand to hand
and be one more in all creation.

I whisper long and low through all the nights
insisting without cease
on my completion.

Ditty: I'm Flying: Opus # 2

I'm flying
like a little girl
with arms out-spread and chocolate on my nose
I'm flying
like a little boy
with everything the pocket won't disclose

I'm flying
like a little bug
with lady-dots a-bouncing on my back
I'm flying
into the Blue
I'll bring you news when I return to you

I'm hopping
on just one leg
I'm not a boy or girl, you'll have to guess
I'm flying
with one leg tucked
and when I land you'll hear me say "I'm quacked"

This ditty
is for the serious folk
who need a bit of laughter in their lives

So sing it, yes
Or hum along
and let your ribs go tickle tickle tong

You're flying
like a whistling swan
You're looking far and wide at all there is
It's grander
than you ever thought
You can't believe what-all you never sought

And what gave you
the wings to fly?
A ditty, just a silly little song
So sing it, hum it, and
we'll come along.

3.
Joys of Age

There was a time

There was a time when it meant nothing to me
that the sky above was filled with stars
that birds sing
that I breathe in, breathe out.

Too busy.

Now, I spread the starry sky, the song of birds
over my memories
I breathe space and silence around each one
and watch my life unfold anew.

Footprints in the Clouds

Two footprints in the clouds
Dissolving.

No need for feet, for us
we are in constant flow
playing with shapes
with ever-forming
configurations.
That's what we do
we play create.

You can't, of course,
quite hear our songs
with ears gone nearly deaf
from motor sounds.
We sing as high and joyous
as you can imagine
with your inner ear.
Join such a sound
with heart beat
and with breath
and there you are,
You're singing, too.

Those foot prints, long dissolved

did lead you here
to song and playfully imagining,
to one great universe in motion
and you, a part of it,
among the joyous ones,
the flying, soaring, gliding, floating ones
And how might that now feel?

Now, there are labels you can give
and stick into a lexicon,
a fun game, too
but not the only one.
That's playing cards
when you could see the world instead,
a world so high and deep and long,
so infinite in all its ever-flowing play.
A nut just fallen from a tree
with one quick wake-your-ear-up twong
can re-awaken, if you're ready,
the songs of glorious clouds
in all your days and nights,
and joining them, your own voice,
bright and clear, and full of joy.

There's a poem coming

There's a poem coming
There's a sad one on the way
I run, I read, I watch a video
and: poom
Tears a-flowing.

There's a poem coming about tears
How they wash me clean
So I can see the world newly bathed
In all its glorious colours.

But now, what's happened to the poem?
Will it come, with sadness gone?
Why yes, it's a poem about sadness
dissolving
No words
The poem is in the seeing.

Now are you glad? Or sad
there's no poem on the way?
Just life, which,
if you're willing to cry
Is a poem

of re-birth in every tear
Of sparkling colour and
soothing gentle motion
In and out of tears
and Joy.

Your Task, Your Joy

Food for the soul
where to find it
when books fail
and television's but a sop
when all the little joys of life
have fled
and all the loves you knew
are seen as failed

Then ask youself
how every step
has led you to this point
and hear the voice
in darkness, speaking low:
this was your path
you chose it all along
you had to learn and
be at odds
with all you learned
so that in time
in this long darkness
you could envision all the past
as learning and
as leading to the moment
of asking what comes next.

Of asking, too, for help
in shaping all the times to come
with loving heart
and with the yearning soul
for peace
To have this blessed rain
of tears
to cleanse, and to rejuvenate
the fallow ground
so that the seeds of joy
can once again be planted there
and bring forth sprouts
which you can tend and nurture

All the while remembering
the lessons learned,
the path on which you came
and with your heart and tears
to nourish, bring forth blossoms
and the wisdom gained in pain.

And then you'll see
the love you sought reborn
to spread its wings
like a gentle mother bird

over all you can create
and bring as gifts
to all the world
so starved for soul
and for the nourishment
which lets it soar and rise
enveloping, embracing all
that comes to you
on this your path, and
ever more in life, in death
and far beyond.

That is the food which every soul
is seeking, ever more
and this, now, is your task,
your gift, your joy.

I'm Croning

Don't bother me with matching threads and buttons,
with make-up, manicures or polished silver,
no time for cooking casseroles and sit-down dinner guests
I'm busy croning.

No time for standing, glass in hand, discussing weather
for writing Christmas cards,
or lists, or tidying,
I'm croning.

The dandelions are pretty,
The hedge is rampant, full of birds
they're watching me
I'm busy croning.

I root among the roots of trees
I hiss in the voice of rapids
I enter the shaman's cave and stir the ashes

I walk barefoot, tenderly, on the unexplored paths
of my inner forest
I step gently into mysterious nooks
and wade in the shifting sands of knowing

There is a dark-water lake

filled with the tears of children
I sit on its shores and sing lullabies
until it sparkles

My pockets are full of seeds
I plant them wherever I see a crack
in the cemented girdle of our mother

I ride the blood stream of my life
to where it joins the ocean of humanity
and beyond, to planetary seas

And the universe so vast and joyous
and all I do, to keep on course, is breathe,
with eyes wide open, like a child.
I'm croning.

And when I'm done,
when I emerge
all feathers bright and wings enormous
then I'll be flying,
yes,
then I'll be soaring.

Gentle Hands

   not as a baby
   not as a child
   as a woman
               not enough
Until now.

Now
I am held
in sleeping as in waking,
embraced by the Love of my life
long dead.

He caresses my ears with the sound of waves and wind and laughter
He holds my face for the gentle touch of raindrops and tears
He shows me the beauty of bark, of a feather,
dancing leaves

and cradles me in his breath.

Now
my petals open to the sun
my seeds are ripe and ready.

This Moment

Leaving behind
the yammering of tasks

Stepping off the path
of merits and grim intent

I fling myself into the ocean of time
this shimmering moment.

Perched

Perched on the edge of my seat
waiting for the next thing
and the next
Missing, all the while
the violet hidden at my feet.

Sitting on the shore of the lake
watching waves come and come
no destination but movement itself
never waiting for arrival or departure.

And what is the edge of the seat
but a slower moving than walking, say
or swimming
nothing holds still,
you can't stop the motion
you can only burp your unwillingness
to be part of it.
Give it up. Give in.
Be willingly, joyfully, in motion.
Be the wave you are
Ongoing for eternity.

Something is coming

Something is coming
I can feel it in my bones.
There's a quiver in the air
aroma of surprise

A cloud just winked at me
with one enormous drifting eye:
"it's coming..."

And here it is,
perched on my window sill:
a Butterfly I've never seen before.

Behold

There's more to me than you might think,
just looking with appraising eyes.
The eyes that gaze and pause a while
and then be smiling, now and then,
those are the eyes to see
the whole of me.

Well, no. The whole of me lies buried deep
and reaches up into the sky
I don't believe I know
the half of me
but I encourage you to try
and I can promise you delight
and much to wonder at
and be in awe of what there might yet be
uncovered.

It's an adventure, after all
to thus embark on seeing me.
It's quite a voyage, sailor man,
with storms and gulls and sails aloft
and always, too, the lullaby
of waves and whispering clouds
and sun or rainbows.

Come, let us anchor heave and be a-sail
upon the seas of love.
Come, let's away and see
what has not ever been discovered yet
until our eyes together
love behold.

Loon Song

The shadows of island hills
lie on the lake, shimmering
a plate falls on the shore –
cushioned by the air so still
and thick with rain,
it lands like a leaf, silently.

Trees are waiting,
holding their breath
distant thunder like a promise,
fingers of clouds
reaching across the night, descending
and now
a loon begins to sing.

Dreaming

Dreaming
not of a white Christmas
not of the wash, hanging clean on a long-gone line
not of waves lapping a meditteranean beach.

I'm dreaming of Joy in the world
of dancing and singing in ever-increasing circles

Dream big, they say, well, it's big, this dream.
It has flowers and doves descending like petals
on all the dancing singing circles
and all the voices, and laughter
rising to meet them.

With never a teardrop,
no hunger, no strife –
it's a dream, after all,
I can picture anything I please.
And in the picturing
with all the colors of the rainbow
there's joy
spreading into every beating heart
to every eye
raised but for a moment
to see the sun or moon above

to make a wish for dreams upon a star
joining, in the skies,
with all the other dreams,
forming like vapour into clouds of Joy
in all the shapes which can be dreamt
and strewn upon the dreaming faces
of those who sing and dance
in circles all around the globe.

You're dreaming, said the reasoned voice.
What a dreamer you are. Are you for real?
Well yes,
but if, of course, your dreams are preferable,
then sit and watch and sneer
while all the dreamers sing and dance.

The choice is yours –
it's only dreaming, after all.

I like my dreams.
Excuse me, but I have to go and dance now
and to sing.

Stillness

Not a leaf is moving
even the clouds are holding still.
Is that possible?
Is all the world holding its breath?

No. There's a moth in motion
a zumming, plop, against the window pane
A solitary moth,
a rocking boat, in rhythmic toc,
a blinking light across the lake.

And through it all –
the toc and plop,
the stillness and the peace:
a singing
high and light and hopeful yet
the singing of our mother
Earth.

Solitude

To sit, listening, until I hear the heartbeat of the universe
to hear its laughter
playful as a child
behold the wonder unfolding in every sound and sight
and far beyond, the vastness of its soul.

To sit in solitude and wonder
if all I hear is true
or if the sounds are calling me
to join a new illusion:
that I, in solitude, am but the blink in the eye of a star,
long gone to other planes
but lingering in long-awaited joy
to streak across the sky and bring to all who see
a moment's rushing breath of life.

I sit in solitude
with all my love
and every sound is in my heart.

Ditty: There's a bug in my Soup: Opus # 3

There's a bug in my soup
It tastes quite good
Crunchy and juicy and very firm, too
I like it, waiter, two more please
And bring the salt, do.

There's a soup on my bugs
I didn't order that
Just bugs and maybe some chips, and wine
That's better, Ah, me...
I do like to dine.

There's a hoof on my heel
How did it get there
'twas on Bessy the cow only yesterday
I can't have just stolen
The hoof off of Bessy
That's just not a nice thing to do
I must go return it
Must tell her I'm sorry
She might be just now
Paraly-zed with worry.

Here, Bessie, your hoof
Don't know how it got switched

Have you seen my new stockings
The ones I had on
Oh, why Bessie, you silly
A cow in silk stockings
Is not at all pretty to see
Now do take them off and
Let bygones be bygones
I'll see you at five, now be good
old Bessie, don't sulk, look alive.

There's a snail in my nostril
A bug in my soup
A hoof on the back of my foot
What next, you might ask me
Whatever comes next
Well, that's up to you, dear
I've had my good fun
And you've been just smiling
So time now to run.
Make your own silly verse
Make your own little smile
Just play and be jolly.
So long.

Acknowledgements

My thanks to Ann Roher for her encouragement and love.

Great thanks to Inanna Publications for choosing to include my book in its illustrious and exciting list, and most especially to Editor-in-Chief Luciana Ricciutelli for making our work together such a pleasure.

The following poems were previously published in the anthology, *Variety Crossing*:

"Unshed Tears" in the third edition
"Joy" and "There was a Time" in the fourth edition
"Something's Coming" in the fifth volume
"Love Behold" in the sixth volume (new title: "Behold")
"Solitude" in the seventh volume
"A Fling" in *Stories That Bind, Variety Crossing 10* (new title "This Moment")
"Joy" and "Gentle Hands" appeared in *Chokecherries* (New Mexico).

Photo: Geoff George

Lilly Barnes is the author of *A Hero Travels Light,* a book of interrelated short stories published in 1986, and of the novel *Mara*, published in 2010. She is also the author of five books for children. She was a freelance Arts Journalist for the CBC for many years, as well as senior script writer for the children's television show *Mr. Dressup* for which she received the 2007 Gemini Award: the Margaret Collier Award for writing, for Outstanding Body of Work. Lilly was married to the late Canadian composer Milton Barnes and has two sons, Micah and Daniel, both musicians. The Literary/Musical event "Jazz for Mara" was based on Lilly's novel *Mara,* with original music composed by Daniel and lyrics by Micah, and was performed by all three, accompanied by Daniel's band. Lilly is now working on a play entitled "Maximum Security." She lives in downtown Toronto, in an old house full of stories and music.